# GUNS AFLOAT

## U.S. Army Riverine Artillery in Vietnam

### By John M. Carrico

SFC, U.S. Army (Retired)

**Guns Afloat**

Copyright © 2014 by John M. Carrico.

Edited by
Glenda A. Gill

Library of Congress Control Number: 2014905865
ISBN-13: 978-0-9794231-4-7
ISBN-10:     0-9794231-4-7
First Edition Softcover

To order additional copies of this book, contact:
**Brown Water Enterprises**

www.brownwater.net

Book cover: A CH-54 Tarhe Helicopter lowers an Airmobile Artillery Firing Platform in South Vietnam.
(USACMH) Insert: Soldiers from Alpha Battery, 3/34th Field Artillery (FA) fire a M102, 105-mm
Howitzer from an Airmobile Artillery Firing Platform in the Mekong Delta, circa 1967. (NARA) Back:
Soldiers from the 3rd BN, 34th FA fire a M102, 105-mm Howitzer from an artillery barge in the Mekong
Delta, circa 1967.

# CONTENTS

# INTRODUCTION AND DEDICATION

I wrote this book as an afterthought of my last published work titled *Waterborne Warriors*, which was about riverine craft used by the United States (U.S.) Army during the Vietnam War. Because of space limitations, I was forced to discard three chapters. Two of those chapters focused primarily on the U.S. Army's riverine artillery, which was created to provide fire support to infantry soldiers operating in South Vietnam's inundated Mekong Delta. Rather than discard those chapters completely, I decided to expand upon them and publish a separate photo history book about this fascinating subject.

I actually began my research on riverine artillery over twenty years ago. In 1993, I had the rare opportunity to serve as an Operations Sergeant on the staff of Lieutenant General (LTG) William G. Pagonis, the Commander of the 21st Theater Army Area Command (TAACOM) in Kaiserslautern, Germany. As an amateur historian at the time, I decided to ask LTG Pagonis to speak with me about his experiences as a Transportation Officer for the 9th Infantry Division (ID) in Vietnam. LTG Pagonis had created a simple staffing tool by using 3 x 5 cards to ask questions or present information for decisions. I quickly received an answer back and an appointment for an office call. During my visit, I was astonished to learn that he actually helped organize the riverine artillery concept for the 9th ID. He showed me his personal photo albums that contained hand drawn sketches of all the artillery barges and modified landing craft, which he allowed me to photocopy. He also allowed me to borrow a video tape that was made during the war that documented his exploits on the rivers in South Vietnam. It provided me with enough historical and personal information to captivate my interests and eventually write this book to pay tribute to the brave soldiers who were part of the mobile riverine artillery units in Vietnam.

# ACKNOWLEDGMENTS

I wish to thank LTG Pagonis for granting an interview and allowing me unlimited access to his personal photo albums. I would also like to recognize the highly professional staff of the National Archives located at College Park, Maryland, and Rich Baker, Historian at the U.S. Army Center of Military History in Carlyle Barracks, Pennsylvania for providing tremendous assistance with my research. Special thanks goes to my editor Lieutenant Coronal (LTC) Glenda A. Gill and my Field Artillery Technical Advisor, Staff Sergeant (SSG) Robert E. Howard II; both who have become very close friends.

# PICTURE CREDITS

United States National Archives and Records Administration (NARA)
United States Army (U.S. Army)
U.S. Army Center of Military History (USACMH)
Ron Snyder
Vietnam Research

# TERMINOLOGY

| | |
|---|---|
| AMMI | Navy construction pontoon |
| AN/MRC | Army-Navy/Mobile Radio Communications |
| APC | Armored Personnel Carrier: an amphibious tracked vehicle used by the Army |
| ATC | Armored Troop Carrier: a heavily modified LCM(6) Navy Landing Craft |
| BDE | Brigade |
| Beehive | Anti-personnel projectile used against troops |
| BN | Battalion |
| CC | Command and Control |
| CDR | Commander |
| Chinook | CH-47 helicopter |
| CO | Company |
| CP | Command Post |
| DIV | Division |
| FA | Field Artillery |
| FDC | Fire Direction Center |
| Four Deuce | 4.2 inch M30 Mortar |
| FSB | Fire Support Base |
| Hootch | Slang used to describe a makeshift dwelling |
| ID | Infantry Division |
| In country | Slang used to describe the Vietnam-theater of operations |
| LCM | Landing Craft Mechanized |
| LZ | Landing Zone |
| MB | Medium Boat |
| Mike Boat | Nickname for the Army's Landing Craft Mechanized, Mark-8 |
| Monitor | A heavily modified and armed LCM(6) Navy Landing Craft |
| MOS | Military Occupational Specialty |
| Mph | Miles per hour |
| MRB | Mobile Riverine Base: a cluster of ships, barges and pontoons to form a floating base |
| MRF | Mobile Riverine Force: forces organized to conduct riverine operations |
| Paddy Platform | 23 square-foot, air-portable artillery platform used in the Mekong Delta |
| POL | Petroleum, Oils and Lubricants |
| PSP | Perforated Steel Planking: used for makeshift runways |
| Skycrane | CH-54 Tarhe Helicopter |
| SOP | Standard Operating Procedures |
| TC | Transportation Company |
| TM | Technical Manual |
| RTO | Radio Telephone Operator |
| RAC | River Assault Craft |
| RVN | Republic of Vietnam |

# Chapter One

## RIVERINE ARTILLERY IN VIETNAM

During the Vietnam War, U.S. combat units faced a significant mobility challenge operating in the Mekong Delta region of South Vietnam. Swamps, rivers and flooded rice fields precluded normal means of transportation to deliver troops and supplies. Helicopters were used very successfully for air mobility in Vietnam. However, to alleviate the ground mobility situation, military planners developed a Joint Mobile Riverine Force (MRF) by combining U.S. Army Infantry elements with U.S. Navy River Assault Craft (RAC) to maneuver and engage the enemy in marshy terrain. The Riverine Assault Force used small armored gunboats to insert soldiers using the rivers and canals as the main mode of transportation since there were virtually no dry roads in the Mekong Delta to use ground vehicles effectively.

An important element for infantry forces to win on the battlefield is the successful use of indirect fire. Artillery is the deadliest and most effective means of close support for soldiers in contact with the enemy. Artillery provides an advantage of overwhelming firepower and it can also reach targets outside of the immediate battle area to disrupt enemy supply lines, escape routes and destroy reinforcements. Normally, artillery must have firm ground to deliver accurate fire. Because the terrain in the Mekong Delta was so wet and unstable, new techniques had to be developed to insure that artillery could be used to support riverine combat operations.[1]

A Radio Telephone Operator (RTO) maintains communications during a search and destroy mission in South Vietnam, circa 1968. Quite often soldiers were required to negotiate open terrain, which dangerously exposed infantrymen, if ambushed. Immediate artillery support was critical for survival on the battlefield to suppress the enemy and allow soldiers to fire and maneuver, or withdraw to safer positions. (NARA)

Troops and equipment were transported to and from combat areas in the Mekong Delta by Navy Landing Craft and Army helicopters. The landing craft were protected by heavily armored gunboats called Monitors, but they were unable to provide sufficient indirect fire support to the soldiers operating on shore. The MRF planners failed to adequately address fire support when developing the force. The original concept called for Navy Armored Troop Carriers (ATC) to transport Army 105-mm Howitzers to an engagement area. The ATCs would also carry trucks as prime movers to offload and position the howitzers. However, this idea proved to be insufficient because the river banks in the Mekong Delta were too steep to lower the boat ramps. This was because tidal fluxuations on the rivers ranged from 5 to 13 feet depending on the time of year.[2] Additionally, the high water table made the ground soft causing trucks to become stuck in the mud and howitzers difficult to traverse and safely engage targets.[3]

Field artillery support for the MRF was initially provided from fixed locations on scarce dry ground that was normally in the close proximity of Vietnamese hamlets. This was not an ideal situation since loud artillery fire disturbed the villagers and made winning hearts and minds more difficult. Riverine artillery needed to be highly mobile and positioned near the immediate battle area to be effective. In December 1966, the Army experimented with firing a howitzer from a Navy Landing Craft. This method was somewhat successful but limitations traversing the gun and stabilizing the boat caused inaccurate fire. Next, the Army tried using pontoons and barges that were more stable on the water and the guns could traverse in all directions, but this also presented other mobility challenges because barges were not self-propelled and needed to be towed by other watercraft. Another innovation explored was the use of airmobile artillery. The Army developed a firing platform that could be airlifted by helicopters and placed in water or swampy terrain to give a stable firing position for field artillery.[4]

All of these approaches to solving the unique mobility challenges in the Mekong Delta lead to the development of America's first mobile riverine artillery unit. Since nothing like this had ever been tried before, tactics and techniques had to be learned by trial and error. Commanders, who lead these elements, were innovators in their own sense by creating doctrine as they engaged a determined enemy traveling along hostile rivers of the Mekong Delta.

The USS Colleton (APB-36) was a Benewah-class barracks ship that formed part of a floating Mobile Riverine Base (MRB). When the MRF was established it had inadequate fire support assets. The creation of mobile riverine artillery solved this deficiency. (NARA)

The second generation Monitor mounted a 105-mm M-49 Howitzer in a turret taken from a Marine Corps amphibious tracked vehicle. The "Heavy" Monitor provided some indirect fire support for the MRF but ground artillery was much more desired by infantry commanders. (USACMH)

The U.S. Navy ATC was a modified LCM(6) with bar armor and heavy weapons added to support infantry. The MRF planners considered using these boats to emplace towed artillery near battle areas but this concept was problematic. One reason was the ramp of the ATC would not always lower far enough to off-load a howitzer as evident in this photograph. Other methods would need to be considered to employ artillery in the Mekong Delta. (NARA)

One of two Navy LCM(6) Landing Craft on loan to the Army's 1099th Transportation Company (TC), Medium Boat (MB) in December 1966. The boat is anchored to the shoreline to fire an M101, 105-mm Howitzer. This method of firing artillery on water proved less than adequate because the boat needed to be stabilized before firing could begin.[5] (USACMH)

The rugged LCM(8) was chosen over the smaller LCM(6) to provide the "push and tow" capability for the riverine artillery barges of the MRF. The 1097th TC (MB) was the Army boat unit given the riverine artillery mission. (USACMH)

A U.S. Army LCM(8) of the 1097th TC (MB) tows an AMMI Pontoon along My Cong River, June 1968. This boat appears to be a Command and Control (CC) Vessel towing a helicopter landing barge fabricated from Navy P-1 and P-2 barge sections. The enemy most likely came to the same conclusion and CC boats were juicy targets on the rivers. (USACMH)

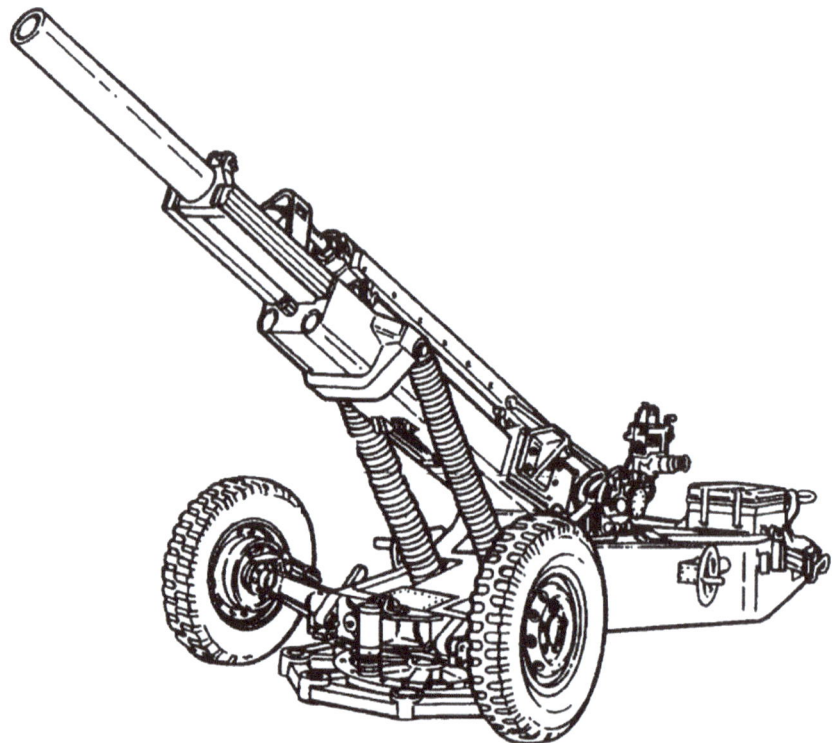

The 105-mm, M102 Howitzer was a lightweight, towed and airborne deployable cannon, which was the primary artillery piece used in the Republic of Vietnam (RVN) by the U.S. Army. (U.S. Army)

# Chapter Two

## UNIT HISTORIES

**9th Infantry Division**

The 9th Infantry Division "Old Reliables" was organized during World War I (WWI), but never actually deployed overseas to see combat in France. The division had a second chance to deploy to Europe during WWII where it was one of the first units to fight in the North African Campaign. After WWII, the 9th ID served during the Cold War in the United States from 1947 to 1962 at Fort Dix, New Jersey, and later at Fort Carson, Colorado. The unit reactivated for combat duties in South Vietnam on 1 February 1966 at Fort Riley, Kansas to serve as the maneuver element of the MRF in the Mekong Delta. The division arrived in South Vietnam on 16 December 1966 and remained until 27 August 1969, when it became one of the first units to depart Vietnam as part of President Nixon's Vietnamization Program. After the war, the Division became "Motorized" and was based at Fort Lewis, Washington. The unit inactivated for the last time in December 1991.[1]

### 3rd Battalion, 34th Field Artillery Regiment

The 3rd Battalion (BN), 34th FA Regiment was activated in 1966 to serve with Division Artillery of the 9th ID in the RVN. The battalion provided artillery support for the MRF in the Mekong Delta. The 3/34th FA earned the distinct title as the first unit in the U.S. Army to have waterborne artillery. The unit employed 105-mm howitzers in combat using prefabricated naval barges and airmobile firing platforms. Bravo and Charlie batteries were stationed on the barges and Alpha battery deployed its artillery into combat using the airmobile platforms. The unit participated in many successful riverine operations until redeploying to the United States in August 1969. The unit remained with the 9th ID until the unit moved to Fort Lewis, Washington in 1972.[2]

### 1097th Transportation Company (Medium Boat)

The 1097th TC (MB) deployed to South Vietnam on 30 May 1965 and was based at Cam Ranh Bay. The unit was attached to the 45th Engineer Group at Vung Ro Bay to help build South Vietnam's second largest deep water seaport. The unit had a combat strength of 180 soldiers, nineteen LCM(8) and one LCM(6) CC vessel. In July 1967, the unit was reassigned to support the 3/34th FA, 2nd Brigade, 9th ID in the Mekong Delta. The new mission for the 1097th TC (MB) was to tow artillery barges along the rivers to provide indirect fire support for riverine infantry conducting waterborne assaults. The unit operated very successfully and developed its own Standard Operating Procedures (SOP) to support riverine combat operations. The unit redeployed to the United States with the 9th ID in August 1969.[3]

# Chapter Three

## ARTILLERY PONTOONS & BARGES

The Army did not have any pontoons that were large enough to carry howitzers, so they had to be borrowed from the Navy. The Army initially used the AMMI pontoon, which was a stable firing platform but it was difficult to move around because of its large size and the draft was too deep to negotiate the small rivers and canals in the Mekong Delta.[1]

An alternative to the AMMI pontoon was the Navy's P-Series Pontoon Barge. There were five basic types of P-Series pontoons designated as P-1 through P-5. The P-Series pontoons were constructed of welded steel cubes that were designed to withstand an internal pressure of twenty-pounds per square inch (psi). Each pontoon section had deck plates covered with a nonskid coating, and all were fitted with two-inch plugged holes for air, drain or siphon connections.[2] The five by seven-foot P-1 pontoon was the most commonly used section and was connected together to form a single floating barge that was ninety-feet long by twenty-eight feet, four inches wide. Connected on each end of the barge were P-2 sections that had sloping bows like a boat to give the barge more maneuverability when being towed.

Between February and April 1967, experiments were conducted in cooperation with the Navy to determine if the P-1 pontoon was a feasible option for employing artillery in the Mekong Delta. Firing tests were performed at Dong Tam under various conditions and the results were highly successful. The 9th ID immediately requested six riverine artillery barges, which were fabricated at Cam Ranh Bay.[3]

The modified P-1 artillery barge could carry two M102, 105-mm howitzers complete with ammunition and the gun crews. Armor plates were added around the sides of the barge for protection. Ammunition storage bunkers were built on each end and living quarters were built in the center. The baseplate of the M102 howitzer was welded to the deck of the barge so the guns could rapidly traverse in any direction.[4]

A riverine firing battery consisted of three barges and five LCM(8) landing craft. Three LCMs were used to push the barges, one was used as a Fire Direction Center (FDC), and the fifth LCM(8) was used to transport ammunition. The firing batteries moved along the rivers supporting MRF operations. If they were ambushed along the way the howitzers would respond with deadly direct fire and small arms to suppress the enemy.[5]

Once the objective area was reached, the barges were pushed into position along the riverbanks and stabilized using grappling hooks and winches. Mooring lines were placed on the shore and adjusted for tidal changes, so the barges would not be caught in the mud during low tide. Aiming posts were set-up on the riverbanks to provide fire direction. The barges provided a stable firing platform and accuracy was just as good as ground-mounted howitzers.[6]

The MRF also had specially designed Mortar Barges. The 9th ID "Four Deuce" battery mounted four, M30, 4.2" mortars on two custom built P-1 barges. The Mortar Barges were manned by infantry soldiers, who were berthed on the northern bank of Dong Tam harbor. During riverine operations and while defending the base at Dong Tam, the unit became quite good at providing counter–fire support. The path of incoming enemy rockets and mortars was detected by radar triangulation, which mathematically calculated reverse trajectories that enabled the Four Deuces to accurately return fire.[7]

Aerial view of a P-1 artillery barge with an Army LCM(8) landing craft pulled alongside in 1968. In June of 1967, the U.S. Army's 1097th TC (MB) was given the mission to transport twelve 105-mm howitzers belonging to two artillery batteries of the 3/34th FA in support of the 2nd BDE, 9th ID in the Mekong Delta.[8] (USACMH)

An interesting photograph showing the relative size of an AMMI Pontoon (left) as compared to a Navy P-1 Barge (right). Because of its size, the AMMI Pontoon was much more difficult to maneuver in the shallow waters of the Mekong Delta. (Vietnam Research)

An AMMI pontoon converted into a floating artillery platform for an M101A1, 105-mm howitzer at Dong Tam, 25 March 1967. Most AMMI pontoons used for riverine artillery only had sandbags for protection. The AMMI Pontoon was a stable firing platform but it could not be easily towed and positioned by small watercraft. (NARA)

The crew of an M101A1 howitzer conducts a fire mission on an AMMI Pontoon in 1967. Notice the wooden frame and sandbags used to protect the howitzer ammunition. The M101A1 howitzer had wheels as did the M102, but the M102 also had a retractable baseplate that could be lowered, which was connected directly to the P-1 Barge to make the cannon more stable and secure when firing. (NARA)

14

barge

Firing port
for direct fire

Armor plate

M102 105-mm howitzer bolted
to deck

Gun
section
bunker

360°fire
capability

barge

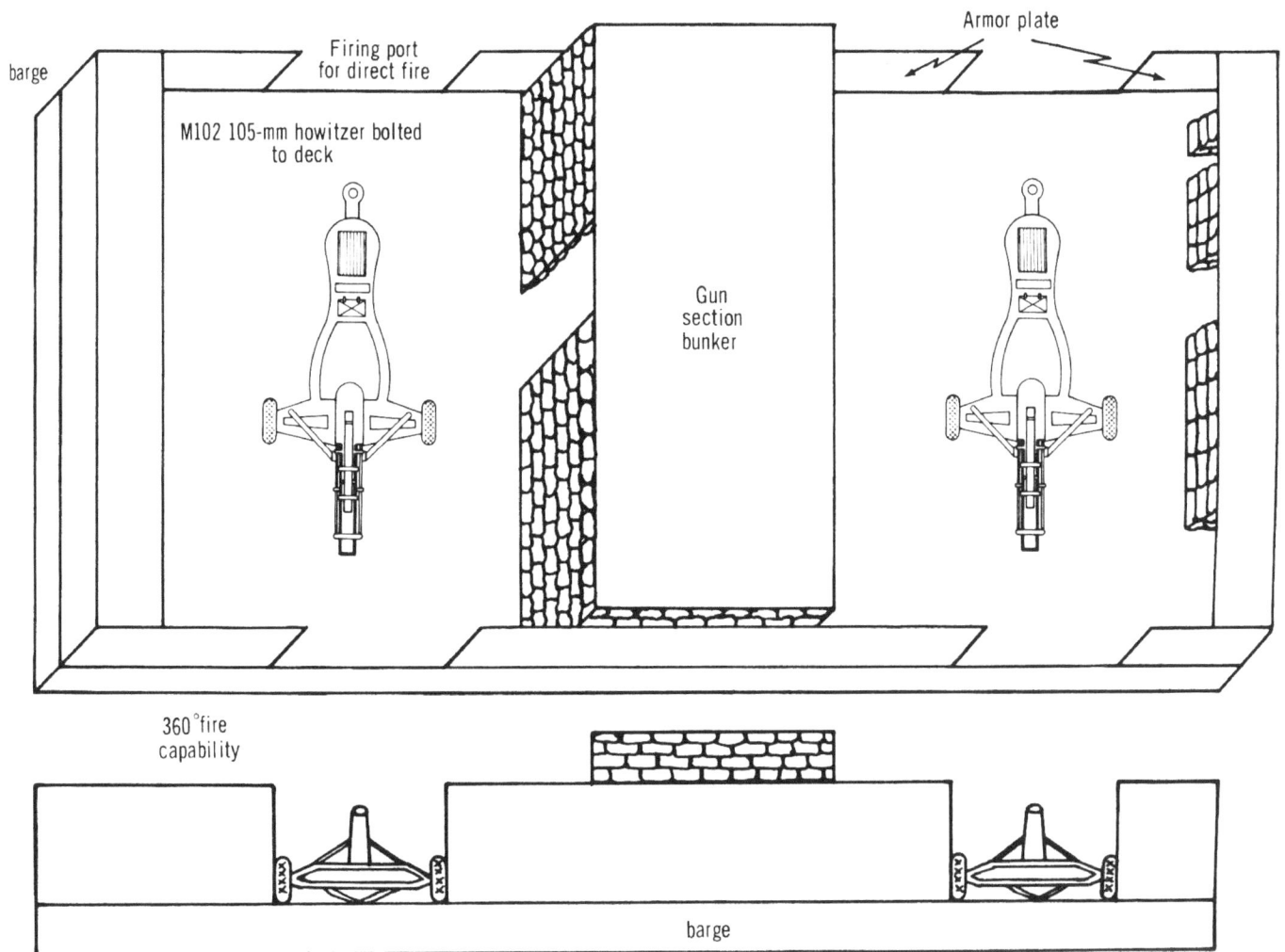

Layout of an artillery barge from a 1972 U.S. Army Technical Manual (TM) for riverine operations. The riverine artillery barge mounted two M102, 105-mm howitzers, ammunition, and living quarters for the gun section. (U.S. Army)

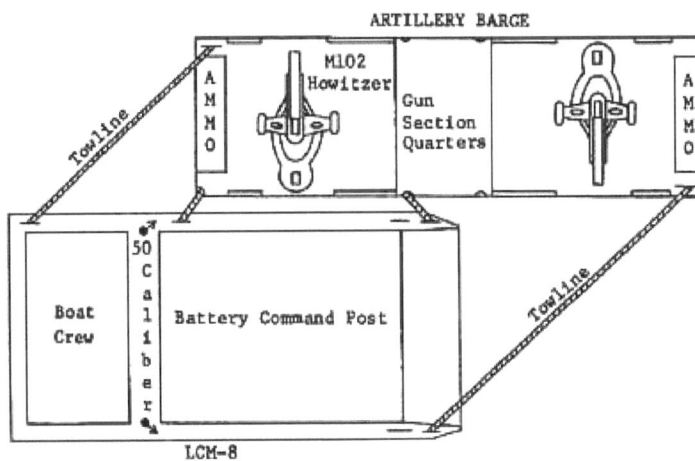

ARTILLERY BARGE

Towline

AMMO

M102
Howitzer

Gun
Section
Quarters

AMMO

Towline

Boat
Crew

50
Caliber

Battery Command Post

LCM-8

A sketch from an Army TM showing how the P-1 barges were attached and towed by LCM(8) Landing Craft. (U.S. Army)

# P-1 ARTILLERY BARGE

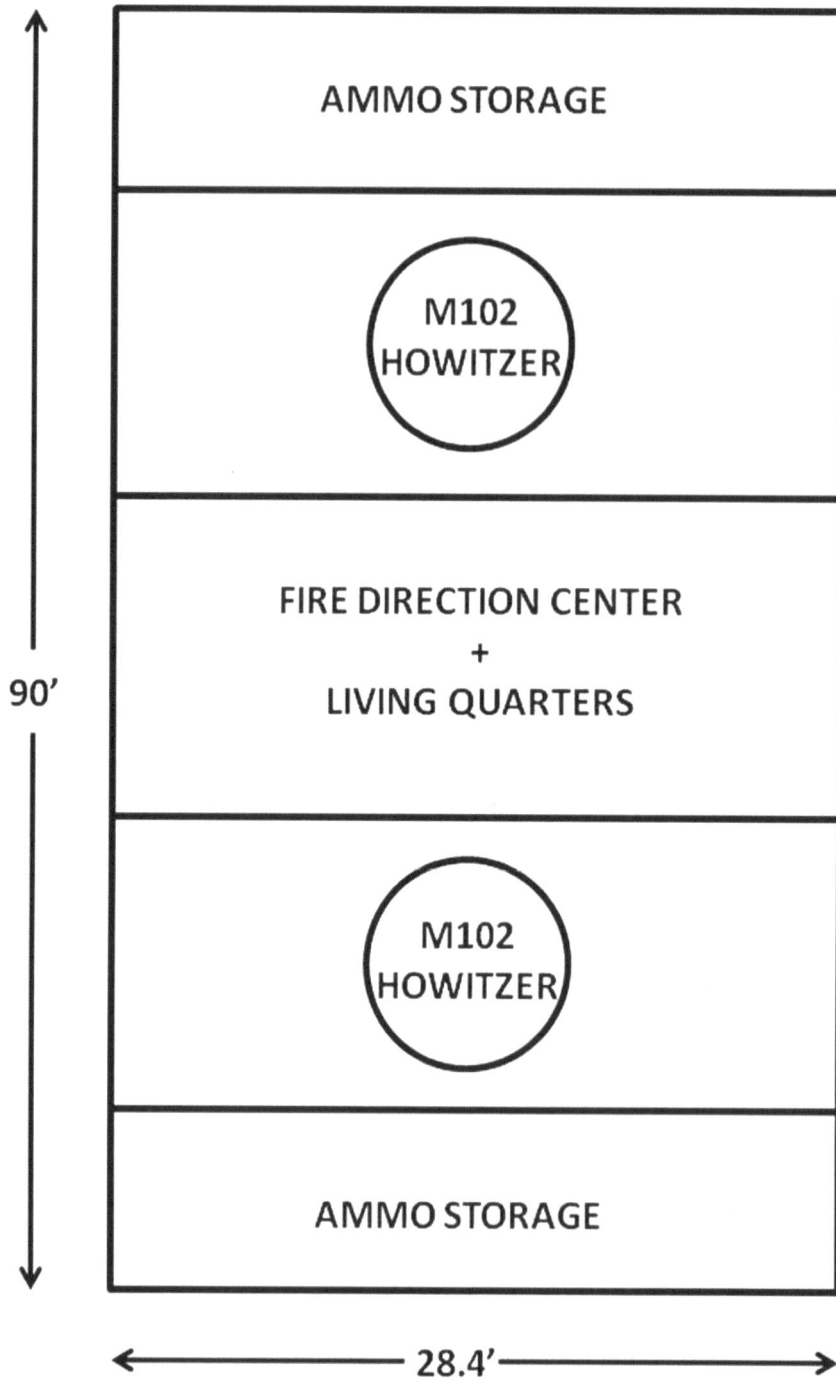

```
                    AMMO STORAGE


                    ( M102
                      HOWITZER )


90'              FIRE DIRECTION CENTER
                          +
                   LIVING QUARTERS


                    ( M102
                      HOWITZER )


                    AMMO STORAGE

                    ← 28.4' →
```

The layout of an artillery barge made from the sketches of LTG Pagonis, who as a Captain commanded the only tactical boat unit in the U.S. Army Transportation Corps. The 1097th TC (MB) was tasked to move riverine artillery around the Mekong Delta using twenty-three LCM(8) Landing Craft.[9] (LTG Pagonis & Author)

P-1 Pontoon

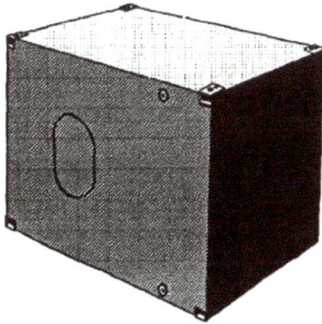

The P-1 pontoon was a watertight cube made from 3/16" steel plating. The deck size of the P-1 was 5'3/8" x 7', and the sides were 5'3/8" high. The P-1 was the most common and widely used section required in every structure of the P-Series Pontoon System.[10] (U.S. Navy)

The P-2 Pontoon Section had the same depth as the P-1, but it had a 7' square deck and a straight-line sloping bow. The welded steel side, end, and deck plates were 3/16" thick and the bow plate was 3/8" thick. P-2 pontoons were used on the bow and stern of riverine artillery barges.[11] (U.S. Navy)

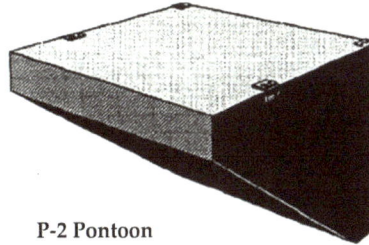

P-2 Pontoon

A P-1 riverine artillery barge is being secured to the shoreline at Dong Tam in preparation for the stand-down of the 9th ID in July 1969. Notice the winch and P-2 pontoon sections attached to the bow. (NARA)

Soldiers attempt to position an artillery barge using lumber, rope and a winch at Dong Tam harbor in July 1969. Notice the sloped bow of the P-2 barge sections to give it more maneuverability. (NARA)

Members of the 3/34th FA use a winch to pull their barges together at Dong Tam in July 1969. Notice the LCM(8) from the 1097th TC (MB) in the background with a "hootch" built on the stern. (NARA)

Members of Bravo Battery, 3/34th FA, 2nd BDE, 9th ID carry a heavy anchor onto shore to stabilize their P-1 pontoon barge in preparation for a fire mission on the My Tho River, 26 September 1967. Riverbanks clear of heavy vegetation were the most preferred anchoring positions. This facilitated helicopter resupply and provided good fields of fire, if a barge was attacked while anchored.[12] (NARA)

Artillerymen of 3/34th FA, 2nd BDE, 9th ID adjusts the aiming sights of their M102, 105-mm howitzer near Dong Tam on 7 July 1969. The M102 howitzer was designed as a replacement for the WWII vintage M101 howitzer system. The frame of the newer M102 was made from lightweight aluminum, which made it ideal for air-borne, airmobile and riverine operations. However, most veteran artillerymen in Vietnam preferred using the old fashioned and reliable M101 howitzer even though it weighed nearly 2 ½ tons–one ton more than the M102 howitzer.[13] (NARA)

Members of the 3/34th FA, 2nd BDE, 9th ID secure their artillery barges to a riverbank with steel cables near Dong Tam on 7 July 1969. Both direct and indirect fire could be delivered from an artillery barge. For indirect fire support, a LCM(8) was run-up on a sloping bank and tied to stumps and trees. The barges were secured against a steep bank in deeper water. In both cases, the same procedures were followed for accuracy and direction of fire.[14] (NARA)

Artillery barges from 3/34th FA, 2nd BDE, 9th ID line up prior to being secured to the shoreline to conduct a fire support mission near Dong Tam on 7 July 1969. Notice the ammunition storage sheds that could hold approximately 750 artillery rounds. Two of these sheds were built on each side for a total of 1,500 rounds per barge.[15] (NARA)

A riverine artillery battery in action on the Mekong Delta in 1968. Notice the crude markings in white paint to direct gun crews where to place their flak jackets, water, and where to exit the birthing area built into the center of the barge. (USACMH)

A riverine artillery gun crew manning their positions on a P-1 pontoon barge in 1968. The M102 howitzer is set to fire in the direct fire mode strait across to the opposite riverbank. The force typically moved at night under the cover of darkness and by sunrise, they were anchored to shore and ready for action.[16] (USACMH)

A gun section of the 9th ID fire a M102 howitzer in 1968. Notice the pocket-patches worn by the artillerymen. Veteran "Redleg" artillerymen preferred using the older M101 howitzer over the newer M102 because the breach was waist high. Loaders would have to bend over in order to insert the 105-mm projectile into the breach of the M102.[17] (USACMH)

A good top view of P-1 artillery barges connected together. The barges were "pushed and pulled" into firing positions by Army LCM(8) Landing Craft. The M102 howitzer had a large roller assembly built into the rear frame that permitted 6400-mil firing capability.[18] (USACMH)

A close-up shot of riverine artillerymen in action. The M102 howitzer had a variable recoil system which eliminated the need for a recoil pit, and was an ideal candidate for mounting on barges and pontoons.[19] (USACMH)

A M102 howitzer mounted on a P-1 barge in action. The M102 could fire 10 rounds per minute and used a variety of aiming sights for different firing conditions.[20] (USACMH)

Ammunition bearers prepare High Explosive (HE) rounds for a fire mission in the Mekong Delta, September 1967. The M102 howitzer fired a variety of projectiles including Illumination, Smoke, Chemical Agent (Tear Gas) and deadly "beehive" anti-personnel rounds.[21] (NARA)

Navy P-1 barges are pushed onto the bank of the My Tho River for a fire mission in September 1967. The artillery barges were normally positioned next to the riverbank opposite of the primary target area, so that the howitzers could fire away from the shoreline. This served two purposes, weapons could be fired at the lowest angle possible to clear obstructions on the far bank, and helicopter Landing Zones (LZs) identified on the near riverbank were not in the direction of fire.[22] (NARA)

Landing craft of Bravo Battery, 3/34th FA, 9th ID enjoy a "stand-down" party in July 1969 after news that the unit is being withdrawn from Vietnam. Notice the heavily modified welldeck and stern. Also visible is a peace sign painted on a banner, which reflects the attitudes of soldiers near the end of the war. (NARA)

# LCM(8) BRIGADE COMMAND POST

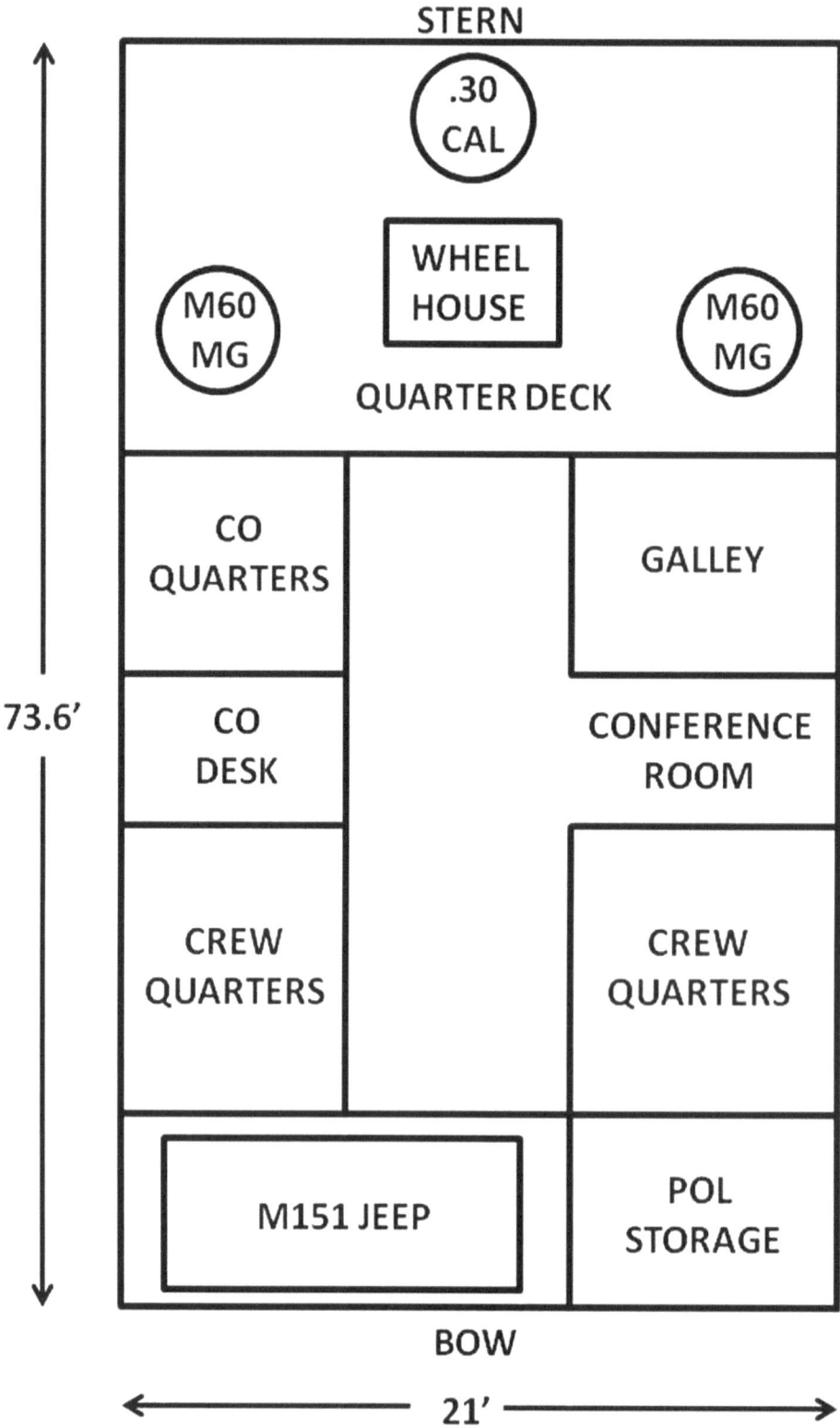

STERN

.30 CAL

WHEEL HOUSE

M60 MG

M60 MG

QUARTER DECK

73.6'

CO QUARTERS

GALLEY

CO DESK

CONFERENCE ROOM

CREW QUARTERS

CREW QUARTERS

M151 JEEP

POL STORAGE

BOW

21'

The layout of a modified LCM(8) Landing craft used as the Brigade CP for riverine artillery. (LTG Pagonis & Author)

# LCM(8) BATTERY COMMAND POST

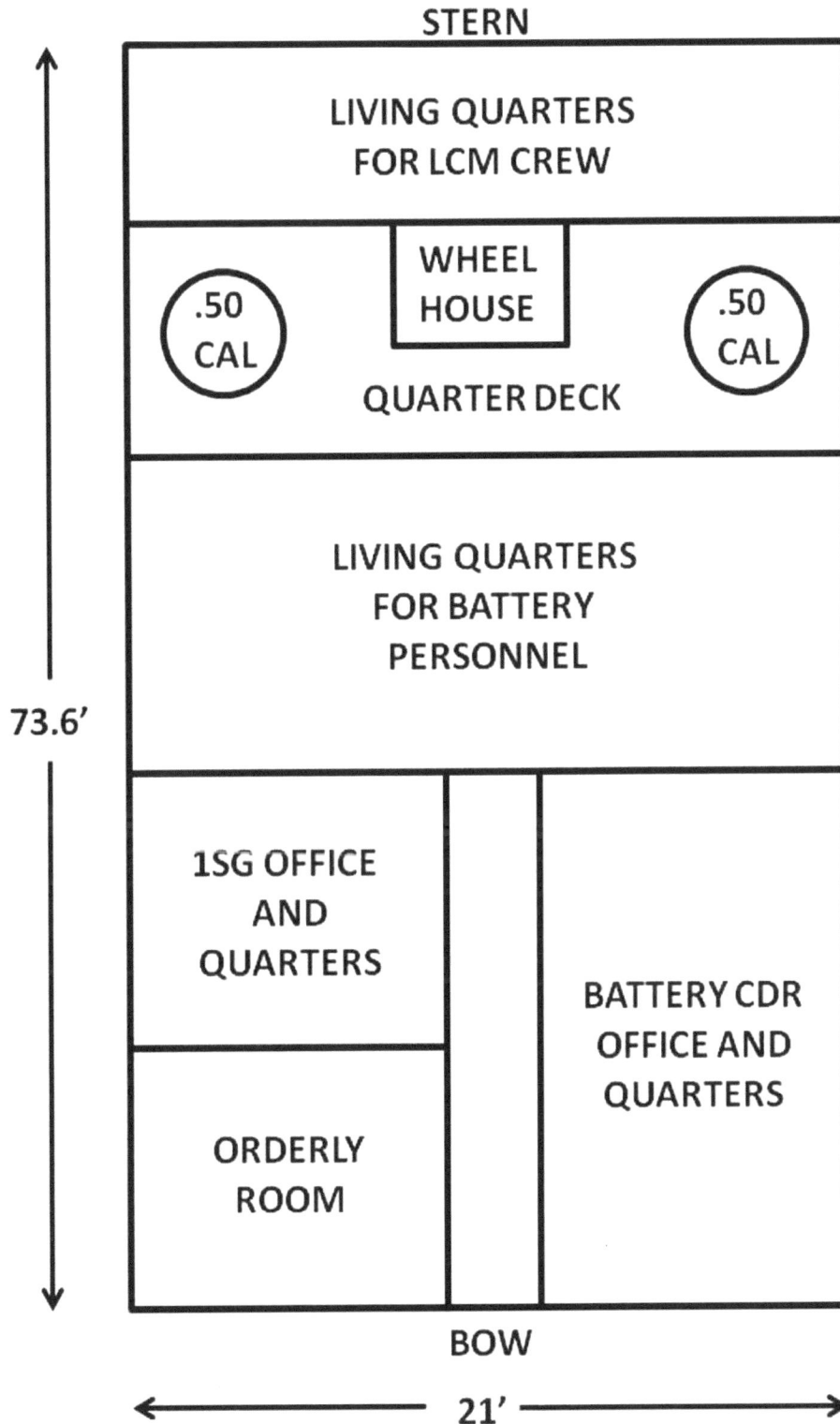

STERN

LIVING QUARTERS
FOR LCM CREW

.50 CAL

WHEEL HOUSE

.50 CAL

QUARTER DECK

LIVING QUARTERS
FOR BATTERY
PERSONNEL

1SG OFFICE
AND
QUARTERS

BATTERY CDR
OFFICE AND
QUARTERS

ORDERLY
ROOM

BOW

73.6'

21'

The layout of a modified LCM(8) Landing Craft converted into a Battery CP for riverine artillery operating in the Mekong Delta. (LTG Pagonis & Author)

A good view of the modified FDC built into the welldeck of an Army LCM(8) Landing Craft belonging to the 1097th TC (MB). Visible is a generator trailer parked next to a communications shelter. The 1097th modified the well decks of other boats in the unit–one was converted into a first aid station, refueler, Prisoner of War (POW) interrogation center, and one boat even had a dayroom built for the crews' morale.[23] (USACMH)

(Left) An Army LCM(8) Landing Craft from the 1097th TC (MB), which was converted into a floating FDC is used to give accurate fire coordinates and triangulations to riverine artillery. The "Fly Swatter" shaped antenna was used with the AN/MRC VHF radio. (USACMH)

# P-1 HELICOPTER BARGE

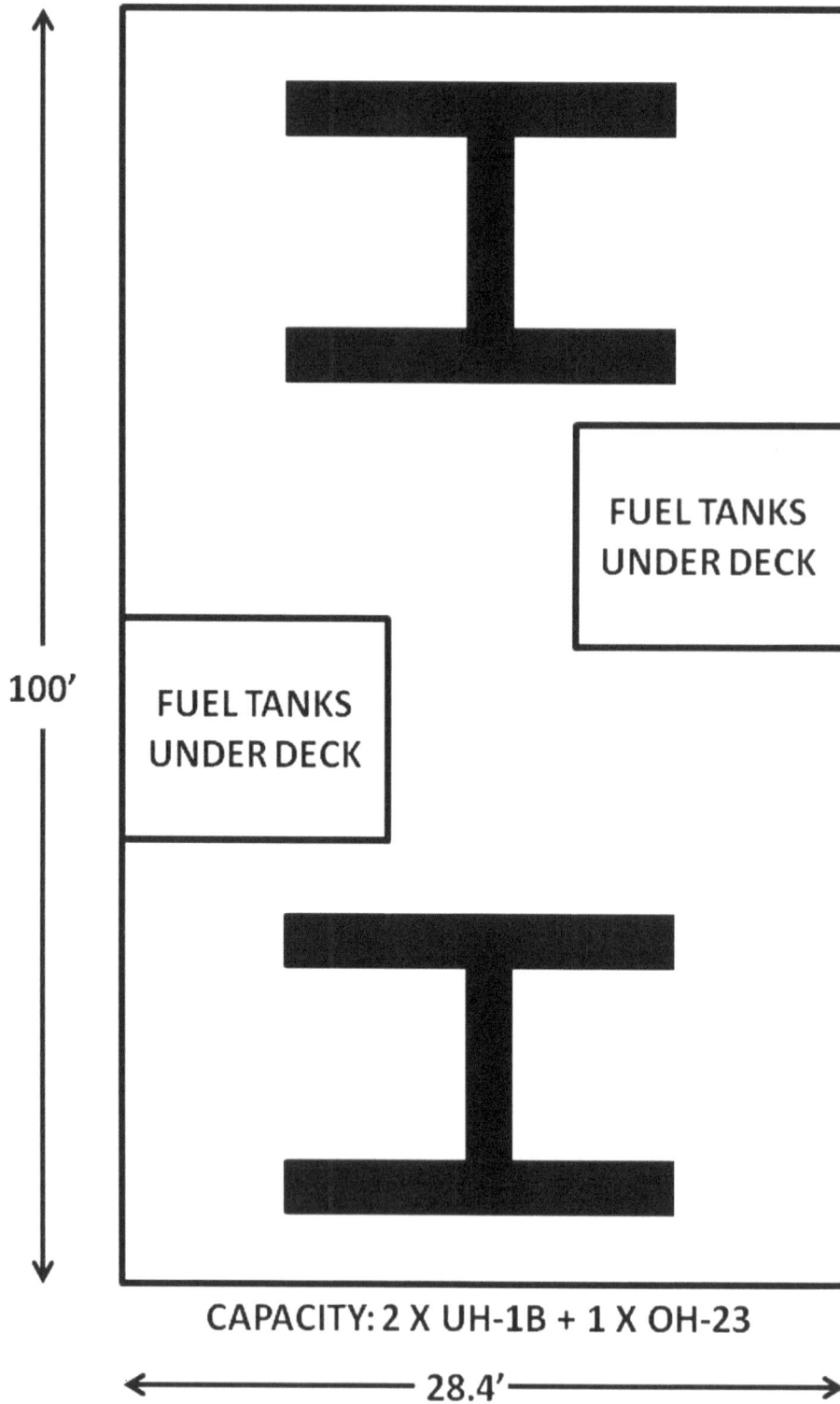

100'

FUEL TANKS
UNDER DECK

FUEL TANKS
UNDER DECK

CAPACITY: 2 X UH-1B + 1 X OH-23

28.4'

A UH-1D Huey from the 9th ID lands on a mobile helicopter barge made from Navy P-1 pontoon sections. The helio-barge was an important asset to the 1097th TC (MB) Command Post (CP) element operating in the Mekong Delta. (NARA)

(Left) A diagram made from LTG Pagonis' sketches of the specially designed P-1 Helicopter Barge. Helicopters could land unimpeded on the barge for a variety of tasks including delivering mail, rations, ammunition and other important supplies. They could also be used to evacuate causalities and provide Petroleum, Oils and Lubricants (POL) to helicopters running low on fuel. (LTG Pagonis & Author)

# P-1 MORTAR BARGE

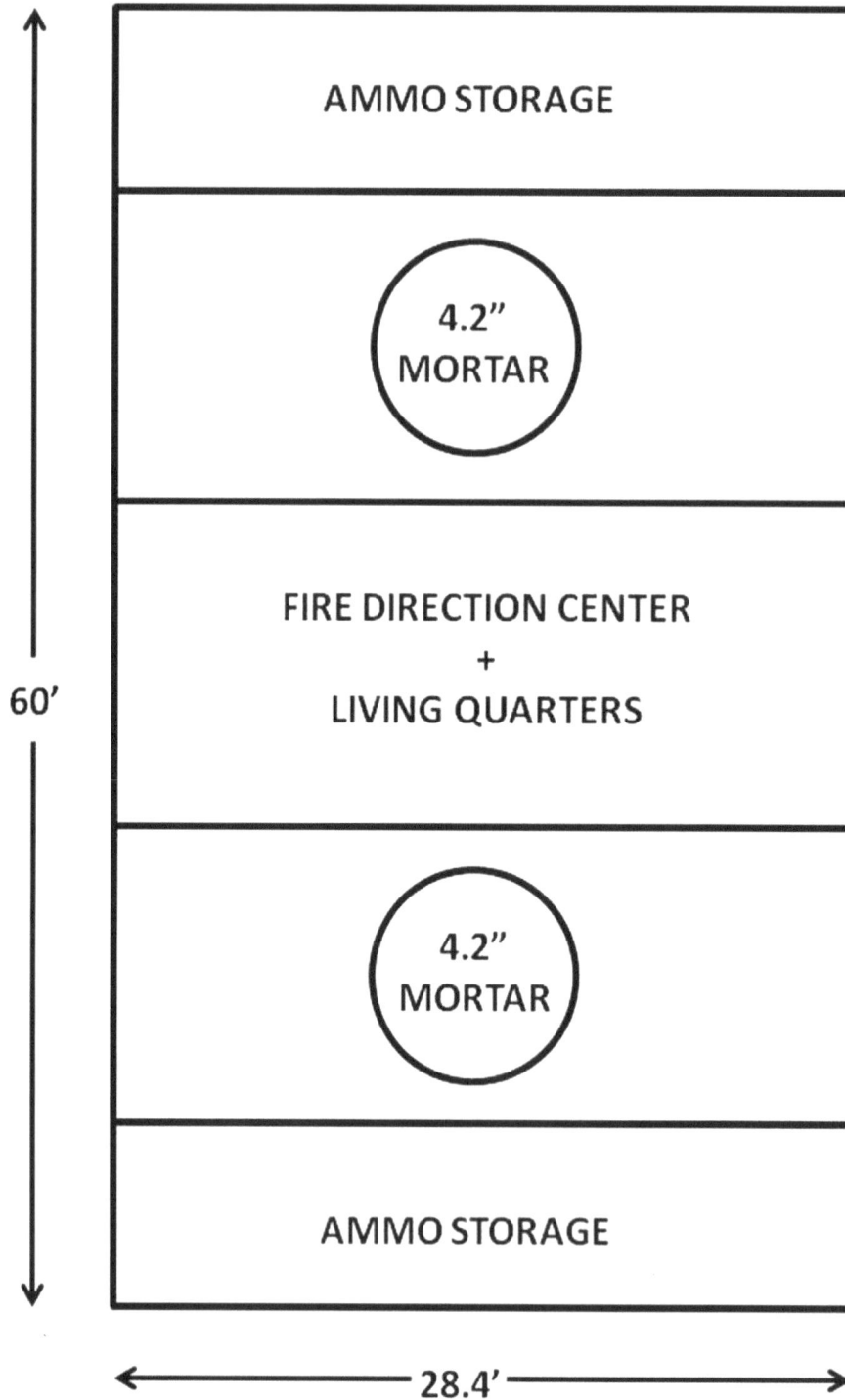

A diagram from LTG Pagonis' sketches of the specially designed P-1 Mortar Barge used in the Mekong Delta. (LTG Pagonis & Author)

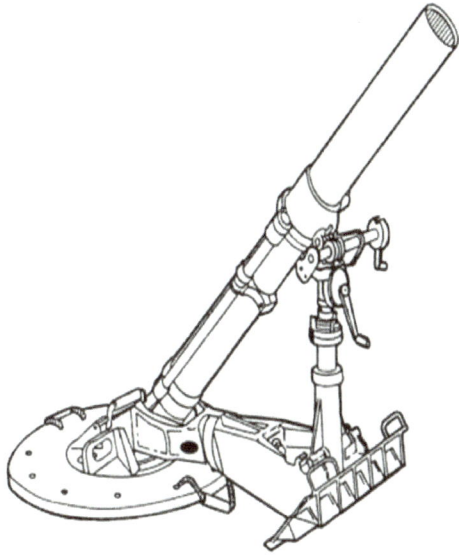

The 107-mm (4.2 inch), M30 was the primary heavy mortar used in Vietnam. The weapon had a high-angle-of-fire and was **muzzle-loaded** with a rifled barrel, which armed projectiles after they left the tube and rotated a number of times a safe distance from the firing position.[24] (U.S. Army)

A "Four Deuce" barge of the MRF is moved into a firing position at Dong Tam by an Army LCM (8) Landing Craft in 1968. Notice the location of the crews fighting gear and flotation vests. (Ron Snyder)

The baseplate of a "Four Deuce" mortar is lowered into position on a P-1 Mortar Barge. Notice the dirt placed inside of the frame and under the baseplate to absorb the recoil of the mortar. When firing the mortar on the dry ground the recoil caused the base plate to shift and crews needed to re-aim the mortar. This caused a delay in the rate of fire, which was not a problem for mortars mounted on barges.[25] (Ron Snyder)

A soldier poses for a photograph standing on the empty base plate of an M30 mortar. Infantry soldiers who held the Military Occupational Specialty (MOS) of 11C were mortar men who crewed the "Four Deuce" barges in Vietnam. (Ron Snyder)

An interesting photograph of a 107-mm M30 mortar mounted on a P-1 Mortar Barge. Notice the truck tire placed under the baseplate on this barge. The tire would absorb much of the recoil. Dirt was placed under the tire to further reduce structural damage to the barge when firing the mortar. (Ron Snyder)

A "Four Deuce" crew preparing to fire their mortar at Dong Tam harbor. The baseplate used for this modification came from the M-106 Self-propelled Mortar Carrier, which was the indirect fire version of the M-113 Armored Personnel Carrier (APC). (Ron Snyder)

# Chapter Four

## AIRMOBILE FIRING PLATFORMS

Another unique invention the Army used to deploy field artillery into the marshes of the Mekong Delta was a specially designed 23-foot steel firing stand nicknamed the "Paddy Platform." These firing platforms were lightweight and air-transportable.[1] Heavy-lift helicopters would pick-up the platforms and lower them into the mud or water to provide a stable firing position. The Paddy Platform could accommodate one 105-mm howitzer, its crew and a limited amount of ammunition. The gun would be put into operation once the platform was level, which could traverse 360 degrees to engage targets in any direction. The platform had four large aluminum "jack-stand" legs with giant footpads that leveled the gun. If any of the legs were stuck in the mud when the platform was being repositioned, the footpad would be disconnected and recovered later.[2]

Initially, two CH-47 Chinook Helicopters were used to put a gun platform into action. One Chinook would position the empty platform while another would carry the howitzer and ammunition. Other platforms could be positioned nearby to store more ammunition, if necessary. The Army soon discovered that Paddy Platforms were aerodynamically unstable when being airlifted. The lightweight of the platform caused it to oscillate during flight and to "float" during descent. On 28 September 1968, a platform severely damaged a CH-47 helicopter causing the pilot to jettison the platform.[3] Major Nick Badovinac, 3/34th Artillery Operations Officer said, "They actually try to fly themselves while going through the air."[4] As an alternative, and always for ammunition storage platforms, eighty rounds of ammunition were loaded on the platform to provide added weight for necessary flight stability.[5] Later, another method to employ the gun platform was adopted by using a single CH-54 Tarhe Helicopter, which could lift both the platform and howitzer together.

A major disadvantage of the platform was that gun crews were completely exposed to enemy fire. Sandbags could be stacked along the edge to provide some level of protection, but it was impossible to construct bunkers or overhead cover. Another disadvantage was the lack of space to store ammunition.[6] In spite of this, Paddy Platforms revolutionized airmobile field artillery tactics and added a new dimension to riverine warfare.

A paddy platform being assembled at Tan An, South Vietnam, 30 September 1967. On the side of the platform were holders for enormous ratchets that were used to level the platform. Notice the M102 howitzer baseplate that is welded to the top of the platform. (NARA)

## ARTILLERY FIRING PLATFORM

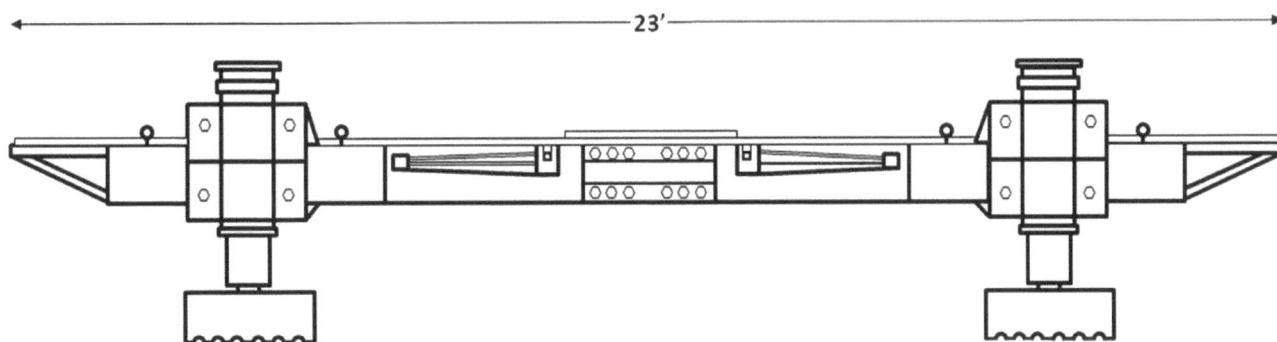

An illustration of the U.S. Army riverine artillery firing platform. The 18 x 23-foot platform was made of light-weight steel, which was air-deployable by heavy-lift helicopters.[7] The platform was given several nicknames like "Paddy Platform," "Paddy Pad" and "Swamp Platform." (Author)

Paddy Platforms being assembled at Tan An, Vietnam in 1967. Notice the holes in the bottom of the platform suspended on the winch. This aided in keeping the platform ultra lightweight and would allow water to drain out when repositioned. (NARA)

Two soldiers of the 9th ID carry one of the retractable legs of a Paddy Platform. Each had four legs that were bolted to the platform and the height of the legs could be adjusted by large pistons. (NARA)

Lieutenant Colonel (LTC) Charles F. Gordon Jr., CDR of 2nd BN, 34th Artillery, 9th ID inspects a paddy platform being assembled at Tan An, South Vietnam, 30 September 1967. The platform is being suspended by empty 55-gallon fuel drums until the large aluminum "jack-stand" legs can be bolted onto the platform. (NARA)

One of the enormous legs of a Paddy Platform is being hoisted, so it can be bolted in position. (NARA)

The leg of a Paddy Platform is being adjusted into position by lining up the two white lines. Notice that the footpads had large holes drilled in them to reduce weight and allow water to drain when being repositioned. (NARA)

A completely assembled Paddy Platform at Tan An, South Vietnam in 1967. Notice the large base plate welded to the middle of the pad to attach an M102 Howitzer. (NARA)

A 9th ID soldier places a safety cable on the leg of a Paddy Platform. This cable ensured the footpad would not be lost if it became separated from the adjustable leg. (NARA)

A CH-54 Tarhe Helicopter lifts an airmobile "Paddy Platform" during a riverine operation in 1968. Notice the giant footpads, where one has become detached and is dangling by a safety cable. (USACMH)

A Paddy Platform being sling-loaded into position by a CH-47 Chinook Helicopter in 1969. Notice the local Vietnamese children playing in the water while observing the big spectacle. The Boeing CH-47 Chinook was a medium-lift **helicopter** capable of carrying a maximum payload of 10,000 lbs. It had tandem, twin-engines and was developed for the Army in the early 1960s to provide "troop movement, artillery emplacement, and battlefield resupply."[8] (USACMH)

A Paddy Platform being sling-loaded by a CH-54 Tarhe Helicopter in 1968. The CH-54 was also called the "Skycrane" because of its heavy-lift capabilities. Notice the attaching points on the platform for the lifting slings. (USACMH)

(Left) A Paddy Platform being lifted by a CH-54 Tarhe Helicopter. Notice how the M102 howitzer is secured to the platform for flight using cargo straps. (NARA)

(Right) A Paddy Platform and howitzer being sling loaded by a CH-54 Tarhe Helicopter in the Mekong Delta. The CH-54 had twin engines and a maximum payload of 20,000 lbs. The CH-54 was built by Sikorsky Aircraft in 1962 and it was named "Tarhe," meaning "The Crane," who was chief of the eighteenth-century Wyandot Native American Indian Tribe.[9] (USACMH)

A Paddy Platform being sling loaded in the Mekong Delta. After the sling was attached, the sling-load team would jump off the platform to avoid being shocked by the helicopters electromagnetic field produced by the rotating blades. (USACMH)

A Paddy Platform in position, Mekong Delta, 1968. Because the platform was extremely light, it had a tendency to float during descent when being airlifted. To resolve this problem an M102 howitzer and or ammunition was transported with the platform for added weight and stability. (USACMH)

A Paddy Platform after it was delivered by a CH-54 Tarhe Helicopter. The gun crew goes into action removing the slings to put the howitzer into operation. Notice that one large foot pad is not connected to the "jack-stand." (USACMH)

A riverine artillery battery in action, Mekong Delta 1968. Perforated Steel Planking (PSP) that was used to create makeshift runways is used here as a bridge to move between platforms. (USACMH)

SSG John Nichols uses a giant ratchet to level a paddy platform at Tan An, 16 October 1967. The ratchet arm connected to the top of the "jack stand" leg and it was turned either clockwise or counterclockwise to raise and lower the platform. (NARA)

Major General (MG) George A. Carver is briefed on the operation of an Airmobile "Paddy Platform" at Tan An on 27 October 1967. Notice the large flash suppresser attached to the muzzle of the M102 howitzer. (NARA)

A Paddy Platform being used to store ammunition at Tan An on 27 October 1967. Notice the limited amount of space and lack of cover, if attacked. This photograph also shows good detail of the howitzer baseplate, which was welded directly to the platform. (NARA)

A M102 105-mm howitzer attached to a paddy platform is being put into operation in January 1969 at Fire Support Base (FSB) Klaw II. Notice the large wheel attached to the end of the howitzer frame, which allowed the cannon to traverse 360 degrees. (NARA)

An Airmobile Paddy Platform in position--the crew of the howitzer is aligning the sights and preparing the gun for a fire mission in the Mekong Delta. These were sometimes referred to "Swamp Platforms" and were designed to give artillery better response time in bad terrain. Alpha Battery, 3/34th Field Artillery was not the only unit in Vietnam to use the platforms. The 2d Battalion, 77th Artillery, 25th ID "Tropic Lightening" also used them in the swampy regions west and south of the Vam Co Dong River near Cu Chi[10] and Delta Battery, 2nd Battalion, 4th Field Artillery Regiment was the first airmobile firing platform unit in Vietnam.[11] Notice the PSP plating in the water to serve as a bridge for solid footing to access adjacent platforms. (NARA)

A M102 105-mm howitzer of the 9th ID in January 1969 at Fire Support Base (FSB) Klaw II, located approximately 65 KM Southwest of Saigon. The deck of the platform had a thick coat of non-skid paint applied to allow for maximum control of the howitzer and so the gun crews would not slip when it was wet.[12] (NARA)

# ENDNOTES

## Chapter One – Riverine Artillery in Vietnam

[1] Funderburk, Raymond E. MAJ. "The Delta." *Octofoil, 9th Infantry Division in Vietnam* (Vol. 1 / Apr-May-Jun / No. 2). Tokyo, Japan: Dai Nippon Printing Co., Ltd., [c.1968]: Page 38.

[2] The Artilleryman, "Mobile Riverine Force," Centennial Edition, Field Artillery School, Fort Sill, Oklahoma, April 1969: Page 20.

[3] Ott, David E. MG. Vietnam Studies: *Field Artillery, 1954–1973*. Washington, D.C.: Department of the Army, 1975: Page 75.

[4] Ott: Pages 75–77.

[5] Richard E. Killblane, *Army Riverine Operations in Vietnam and Panama* (unpublished): Page 7.

## Chapter Two – Unit Histories

[1] Wikipedia "9th Infantry Division" (online).

[2] Unit History "The 34th Field Artillery" (online).

[3] The History of the 1097th Transportation Company (online).

## Chapter Three – Artillery Pontoons & Barges

[1] Ott: Page 77.

[2] Navy Steelworker, Volume 02, Chapter 10 - Pontoons (online): Page 10-1.

[3] The Artilleryman: Page 22.

[4] Ott: Page 77.

[5] Ott: Page 79.

[6] Ott: Page 80.

[7] Dong Tam Harbor (online).

[8] Killblane: Page 17.

[9] The Artilleryman: Page 22.

[10-11] Navy Steelworker (online): Page 10-1.

[12] Ott: Page 79.

[13] Wikipedia "M102 Howitzer" (online).

[14] Hay, John H. Jr. LG. Vietnam Studies: *Tactical and Materiel Innovations*. Washington, D.C.: Department of the Army, 1974: Page 73.

[15] The Artilleryman: Page 22.

[16] The Artilleryman: Page 23.

[17] Wikipedia "M102 Howitzer" (online).

[18-20] TM 9-1015-234-10: Pages 16-17.

[21] TM 9-1015-234-10: Pages 205-206.

[22] Ott: Page 80.

[23] Killblane: Page 18.

[24-25] Wikipedia "M30 Mortar" (online).

# Chapter Four – Airmobile Firing Platforms

[1] Tropic Lightening News "Mobile Paddy Platform"(online).

[2] Ott: Pages 75–76.

[3] *Operational Report of the 9th Infantry Division Artillery for period ending 31 October 1968.*
Declassified MACV Command Historians Collection. (USACMH): Page 13.

[4] Pacific Stars and Stripes, Aug 1968.

[5] MACV: Page 14.

[6] Ott: Page 76.

[7] Tropic Lightening News "Mobile Paddy Platform"(online).

[8] Wikipedia "Boeing CH-47 Chinook" (online).

[9] Wikipedia "Sikorsky CH-54 Tarhe" (online).

[10] Tropic Lightening News "Mobile Paddy Platform"(online).

[11] Togetherweserved.com "1967-1968, 2nd Battalion, 4th Field Artillery Regiment/D battery Album"(online).

[12] Tropic Lightening News "Mobile Paddy Platform"(online).

# BIBLIOGRAPHY

## Published Sources

Funderburk, Raymond E. MAJ "The Delta." Octofoil, 9th Infantry Division in Vietnam (Vol. 1 / Apr-May-Jun / No. 2). Tokyo, Japan: Dai Nippon Printing Co., Ltd., [c.1968].

Hay, John H. Jr. LG. Vietnam Studies: Tactical and Materiel Innovations. Washington, D.C.: Department of the Army, 1974.

Ott, David E. MG. Vietnam Studies: Field Artillery, 1954–1973. Washington, D.C.: Department of the Army, 1975.

## Unpublished Sources

Headquarters Department of the Army, TM 9-1015-234-10, Operator's Maintenance Manual, Howitzer, Light, Towed:105-MM, M102., Washington, DC, 19 August 1985

Hines, Les., Pacific Stars and Stripes article on 3/34th Artillery, 9th ID, 21 August 1968.

Killblane, Richard E., Army Riverine Operations in Vietnam and Panama.

Operational Report of the 9th Infantry Division Artillery for period ending 31 October 1968. Declassified MACV Command Historians Collection. (USACMH)

The Artilleryman, "Mobile Riverine Force," Centennial Edition, Field Artillery School, Fort Sill, Oklahoma, April 1969.

## Online Sources

Dong Tam Harbor
[26 January 2014] <http://www.gingerb.com/vietnam_dong_tam_harbor.htm>

Navy Steelworker, Volume 02, Chapter 10 - Pontoons
[23 January 2011] <http://www.tpub.com/content/construction/14251/css/14251_257.htm>

The History of the 1097th Transportation Company
[1 February 2014] <http://www.angelfire.com/pa2/Panama2Hot/1097th_History.htm>

Wikipedia "9th Infantry Division"
[1 February 2014] <http://en.wikipedia.org/wiki/9th_Infantry_Division_%28United_States%29>

Wikipedia "M30 Mortar"
[31 January 2014] <http://en.wikipedia.org/wiki/M30_107_mm_Mortar>

Wikipedia "M102 Howitzer"
[23 January 2011] <http://en.wikipedia.org/wiki/M102_howitzer>

Wikipedia "Boeing CH-47 Chinook"
[30 January 2011] <http://en.wikipedia.org/wiki/Boeing_CH-47_Chinook>

Wikipedia "Sikorsky CH-54 Tarhe"
[30 January 2011] <http://en.wikipedia.org/wiki/Sikorsky_CH-54_Tarhe>

Unit History "The 34th Field Artillery"
[1 February 2014] <http://www.angelfire.com/ca5/militaryhistoryus/history.html>

Vietnam Research
[1 February 2014] <http://vietnamresearch.com/mrf/mrf2.html>

Tropic Lightening News "Mobile Paddy Platform"
[2 February 2014] <http://www.25thida.com/TLN/tln4-42.htm>

Togetherweserved.com "1967-1968, 2nd Battalion, 4th Field Artillery Regiment/D Battery  Album"
[23 March 2014] <http://army.togetherweserved.com>

# ABOUT THE AUTHOR

John M. Carrico is a twenty-year U.S. Army veteran, who served as an airborne-infantryman until he retired as a Sergeant First Class in 2004. He is currently serving as a Force Deployment Specialist for United States Forces Korea (USFK) in Seoul. John earned his Associate of Arts degree from the University of Maryland in 2004, authored two history books titled, *Vietnam Ironclads* and *Waterborne Warriors*. He has also produced several short documentary films about the Vietnam War. His hobbies include collecting militaria and restoring antique military vehicles.